hide
this
italian
book

Berlitz Publishing/APA Publications GmbH & Co. Verlag KG
Singapore Branch, Singapore

Hide This Italian Book

Contacting the Editors
Every effort has been made to provide accurate information in this
publication, but changes are inevitable. The publisher cannot be
responsible for any resulting loss, inconvenience or injury. We would
appreciate it if readers would call our attention to any errors or outdated
information by contacting Berlitz Publishing, 193 Morris Avenue,
Springfield, NJ 07081, USA. email: comments@berlitzbooks.com

First Printing: Fall 2005
Printed in Canada

ISBN 981-246-653-3

Writer: Nadja Rizzuti
Editorial Director: Sheryl Olinsky Borg
Senior Editor: Juergen Lorenz
Editors: Lorraine Sova, Francesca Romana Onofri, Eva Betz,
        Alexandra Desbalmes
Cover and Interior Design: Wee Design Group
Illustrations: Kyle Webster, Amy Zaleski

INSIDE

THE INITIATION

Admittance to Italian culture requires more than just knowing a handful of expressions. If you really wanna get in, you've gotta know slang, street speak, and swear words. Hide This Italian Book has what it takes so you can talk the talk. No grammar lessons, verb conjugations, or any rules here—just the language that's actually spoken in Italy today—from the most intimate encounters (and, yeah, we're talking sex) to technology know-how (e-mail, IM, text messaging).

stuff you gotta know

It's assumed you already know a little bit of the Italian language. Most of the expressions provided can be applied to both guys and girls. You'll see ♂ if the word or phrase can be applied to guys alone and ♀ when it's for girls only.

In case you're uncertain about how to pronounce something in the book and don't want to sound like a fool, go on-line: **www.berlitzpublishing.com** and listen up. You may want to lower the volume...

watch out for...

We've labeled the hottest language with a thermometer, so you can easily gauge just how "bad" the expression really is. You'll see:

🌡 These are pretty crude and crass—use with caution (or not).

🌡 Ouch! Be very careful! Totally offensive, completely inappropriate, and downright nasty terms are labeled with this symbol.

We're dealing with real-life Italian in this book and, therefore, we tell you what the closest English equivalent is—so you know <u>when</u> to use each word, phrase, or expression.

You'll also find these features throughout the book:

Un-Censored Slang that's really vulgar or shocking

FACT Cool facts that may seem like fiction

the Scoop Tips on what's hot and what's not

finally

You know that language is constantly changing—what's in today may be out tomorrow. So, if you come across anything in this book that's no longer said, or learn a cool expression that hasn't been included, let us know; we'd love to hear from you. Send us an email: **comments@berlitzbooks.com**. We'll add any hot new expressions to our website—go to **www.berlitzpublishing.com** to check it out.

This book isn't labeled **Un-Censored** for nothing! This isn't the language you wanna use around your boss, relatives, or your new boy- or girlfriend's parents...got it? The stuff that's in here is pretty hot. If you wanna say it in public, that's up to you. But we are not taking the rap (like responsibility and liability) for any mistakes you make—these include, but are not limited to, verbal abuse, fist fights, smackdowns, and/or arrests that may ensue from your usage of the words and expressions in *Hide This Italian Book*.

1 BASIC EXPRESSIONS

*E*verything you need to meet and greet in Italian.

◆ say hello and good-bye
◆ ask what's up

make the first move

Tired of the plain "Ciao"? Try one of these other ways to say Hi!

Ciao! Come va?
Hi, how are you?
Simple but still very popular.

A bello! ♂ A bella! ♀
Hey beautiful!
You'll hear this a lot a lot in southern Italy. If you want to sound like a local, shout it.

Ma guarda chi si vede!
Look who's here! (Literally: Look who is to be seen!)
Say it when you bump into someone you haven't seen in a long time. This includes long-lost "boyfriends" or "girlfriends".

Ma guarda chi c'è!
Look who's here!
Say it with enthusiasm and show your surprise.

In Italy, people traditionally greet each other by shaking hands and with a kiss on each cheek. Nowadays, this is done only with relatives and the elderly. Want to be fashionable? Drop the handshake and just kiss on each cheek. Afraid to get too close? A handshake is a safe, though standard, alternative to puckering up.

how're ya?

The best ways to ask How you doin'? *and the right responses.*

– Come andiamo? How's it going?
– Bene grazie. Good, thanks.

– Tutto bene? Is everything fine?
– Tutto a posto. Everything's OK.
"Tutto bene" is an elegant way to ask how someone is.
Hipsters would prefer "tutto a posto", which is less formal.

– Hey! Come ti va la vita? Hey! How's life?
– Sto da favola! Wonderful! (Literally: I'm in a fairy tale!)

– Hey, come butta? Hey, how're things?
– Butta bene / male. Things are looking good / bad.

– Allora…? Che si dice? So…? What's up?
or
– Che mi racconti? What's going on?
– Sto di merda. I feel like shit.

– Allora… novità? So…what's new?
– Guarda, sto da panico. Well, I'm totally stressed.
or
– Guarda, sto da Dio. Well, I feel divine.

– Come stai? How are you?
– Sto… / Si tira avanti… I'm getting by…

– Come va la vita? How's life?
– Così così. / 'nsomma. So-so.

catch ya later!

Going so soon? Don't be rude—say good-bye.

Vado... Ci si becca in giro.
I'm goin'... We'll see each other around.
This one is sarcastic—for when you don't want to see someone.

Ci sentiamo!
Let's stay in touch! (Literally: We'll hear from each other!)

Fatti sentire / vedere, mi raccomando!
Call me! / Come see me!
Say this to someone you'd like to see again.

Allora... ci si vede!
So...see you!
Say this when you've already made plans to meet up later.

Alla prossima.
See you again.
The classy way to say bye to a friend you'd like to see again.

Vado verso casa... A dopo!
Goin' home... See you later!
Reserve this expression for your closest friends.

Allora... stammi bene.
So...take care.
Say it to someone who needs TLC.

You've seen the word "allora" used quite a bit. "Allora...", So..., or Well..., is
the perfect filler. Use it when you're gathering your thoughts, when you need
a pause, or when you want to sound like a local. It's also the perfect start to
a question and an ideal way to change the topic of conversation.

2 from HOOKING UP to BREAKING UP

*W*hether you're looking to turn on the charm or turn away an unwanted advance, have the expressions you need on the tip of your tongue.

- ◆ come on to someone
- ◆ flatter and flirt like a pro
- ◆ reject a loser

pick-up lines

Don't miss an opportunity to approach that guy or girl you're into because Italian has got you tongue-tied. Practice these fool-proof pick-up lines and you're guaranteed to score.

Vuoi bere qualcosa?
Would you like a drink?

The tried and true line that seems to work.

Scusa... hai da accendere?
Excuse me,...do you have a light?

The best way to spark a conversation without committing yourself.

Ma... non ci siamo già visti prima?
But...haven't we met before?

Arch an eyebrow, tilt your head—this one may be believable.

Vuoi ballare?
Do you want to dance?

You've got the moves, right?!

The typical pick-up...

— **Scusa... Non ci siamo già visti prima?** Excuse me... Haven't we met before?

— **Dipende... Che giri hai?** It depends... Where do you hang out? (Literally: What are your circles?)

or

— **Scusa ma sto aspettando qualcuno!** Sorry, but I'm expecting someone.

These pick-up lines are often used by guys; they're cheesy, but also great for some laughs. And who knows? They may work for you!

Scusa… posso dirti che hai degli occhi bellissimi?
Excuse me,…can I tell you that you've got beautiful eyes?
It's not just your eyes that he likes.

Q: Anna? Anna?
A: Non sono Anna… I'm not Anna…
Just calling out a random girl's name may actually get you digits!

Hai da fare per i prossimi 100 anni?
Doing anything for the next 100 years?
He's ready for marriage—are you?

you flirt!

Is he or she hot?

Quella tipa è…	That girl is…
una gran figa*	really sexy.
una gran gnocca*	
bona da paura.	good (in bed).
uno schianto.	a knockout.
Quel tipo è…	That guy is…
un sano della Madonna.**	really good-looking.
un figo da paura.	a hot, cool guy.
un gran manzo.	a great guy. (Literally: a great bull)

*Guys may talk about a girl being a "figa", literally, fig, or "gnocca", literally, a potato dumpling, among themselves, but would never say it to a girl's face; it can be derogatory.

**Use "della Madonna" (literally: of the Madonna) to describe something or someone—and bring it, him, or her to a higher level…

Un-Censored

Food + sex = "figa". Some speculate that "figa", a northern Italian variant of "fico", fig, became a slang word for vulva *because of the similarities in shape between the two. Don't use the term liberally: it's vulgar in some regions of Italy. Try not to confuse "figa" with "fico" or "figo" —both of which mean* cool!

flattery

Make her or him feel special.

For her:

Franca, sei…	Franca, you're…
speciale.	special.
dolce.	sweet.
bellissima.	incredibly beautiful.

For him:

Mauro,…	Mauro,…
sei speciale.	you're special.
sei troppo forte.	you're really amazing. (Literally: you're too strong)
non sei come gli altri.	you're not like the other guys.

flat-out refusals

Don't want to deal with that pushy guy? Try these…

No, guarda, stasera non è proprio serata.
I'm not in the right mood tonight.
A subtle way to say no thanks.

Scusa, ma sto aspettando qualcun altro.
Sorry, but I'm expecting someone.
It doesn't have to be true.

Evapora!
Disappear! (Literally: Evaporate!)
Clear and to the point!

Lasciami in pace!
Leave me alone!
Brutal, but sometimes it's the only way to get rid of somebody.

Ho di meglio da fare.
I have something better to do.
Snobbish, but it'll work.

Guarda… puoi andare!
Look…you're excused!
He's not good enough to even be in your presence.

Fa / Fai dei metri!
Take a hike! (Literally: Do some meters!)
He probably needs the exercise.

Looking to score? Be prepared for this…

– **Sai che sei proprio figa?** You know, you're really hot?
– **Senti… Fai dei metri!** Listen up… Take a hike!

2GOOD4U

Definitely not interested? Try one of these:

È uno/a…	He/She is a…
sfigato/a.	loser.
cesso.	scumbag. (Literally: a toilet)
mostro.	monster.

Un-Censored

Do you think he or she's really ugly? Doesn't have a personality? Here are some expressions you can use when there are several things—in addition to appearance—you can't stand:

Guarda che…	Look, what a/an…
schifo d'uomo.	repulsive man.
puttaniere. ♂	slut. (Literally: a man who sleeps with prostitutes)
cozza. ♀	dog. (Literally: mussel)
scorfano. ♀	dog. (Literally: scorpion fish)
chiavica. ♀	dog. (Literally: drain, sewer)
puttanella. ♀	little whore.

gettin' dumped

Breaking' it off with class…

Lei…	She…
ha chiuso con lui.	ended it.
lo ha mandato a quel paese. 🌡	sent him packing.
lo ha mandato affanculo. 🌡	told him to stick it up his ass.

breaking up

Fallen out of love? Here are some of the best ways to break it off.

Ho bisogno di tempo per riflettere.
I need time to think about it.
In fact, it's the beginning of the end!

È finita.
It's over between us.
That's right!

È meglio farla finita.
It's better to break up.
It's a gentle way to let someone down.

Rimaniamo amici.
Let's just be friends.
Say it if you mean it!

Con te ho chiuso!
I'm over you! (Literally: I closed with you!)
Give him or her some closure.

 **LOVE and SEX**

There is a reason why the saying "Italians do it better" is so popular.

◆ *get romantic—from kissing to sex*
◆ *the best ways to say we did it*
◆ *virgin or slut?*

in the mood for love?

The expressions you need to tell your love story.

Havin' Fun

Abbiamo una tresca.
We're having an affair.
Nothing serious, right?

Ci facciamo delle storie. NORTHERN ITALY
We're just seeing each other. (Literally: We have some stories.)
Say it when things aren't that serious—yet.

Gettin' Serious

Ci stiamo frequentando. / Stiamo uscendo.
We're going out.
Whether you've been going out for two weeks or two years, use this expression to make sure everyone knows you're exclusive.

È il mio ragazzo. / È la mia ragazza.
He's my boyfriend. / She's my girlfriend.
True love?

And Finally…Sex

Siamo stati a letto insieme.
We went to bed. (Literally: We were in bed together.)
It's pretty obvious, right?!

hot n' heavy

It's about havin' a good time—from kissing to making love.

Ho una gran voglia di baciarti.
I'm dying to kiss you.

Un bacino, per favore…
A little kiss, please…

Mi piaci da morire.
I adore you.

Ho voglia di te.
I want you.

Voglio fare l'amore con te.
I want to make love to you.

sweet talk

Need a pet name for your lover? Try one of these.

Mi dai un bacio,…	Give me a kiss,…
tesoro.	my treasure.
topolina. ♀	my dear. (Literally: little mouse)
luce dei miei occhi. ♀	my sunshine. (Literally: light of my eyes)
passerotto. ♀	my little bird. (Literally: sparrow)
bimba. ♀	baby.
cucciolo/a.	my darling. (Literally: puppy)
dolcezza. ♀	honey. (Literally: sweetness)
piccola. ♀	my little one.
stella. ♀	my love. (Literally: star)
patatina. ♀	my sweetie. (Literally: small potato)
ciccio/a.	my dear. (Literally: fat)

Un-Censored

There are many different ways to say "making love", and some of them can be downright dirty. Guys: don't say these to your girl. These expressions are restricted to the locker room!

Mi piace un casino...	I'm crazy about...
scopare.	@#&!ing. (Literally: sweeping [with a broom])
trombare.	having casual sex. (Literally: playing the trumpet)
chiavare.	screwing.
fottere / ciulare.	@#&!ing. (Literally: swiping)

countless ways to say we did it

Abbiamo passato la notte assieme.
We spent the night together.
Very elegant and tactful.

Abbiamo fatto sesso.
We had sex.
Right to the point.

È successo quello che doveva succedere.
And what was meant to happen, happened.
Destiny...

Abbiamo trombato come ricci.
We @#&!ed like rabbits. (Literally: We @#&!ed like hedgehogs.)
Challenging night, wasn't it?

Finalmente me l'ha data!
Finally she surrendered! (Literally: She finally gave me her vagina!)
Satisfied?

virgin or slut?
gentleman or gigolo?

Say it this way.

Lei è…	She is…
una brava ragazza.	a good girl.
una ragazza a posto.	a respectable girl.
una suora.	a nun.
una santarellina.	a false saint.
una ragazza di facili costumi.	a slut. (Literally: a girl of easy virtue)
una bomba da sesso.	a sex bomb.
Lui è…	He's…
un cavaliere. **un gentleman.**	a gentleman.
un bravo ragazzo.	a good guy.
un ragazzo per bene.	a respectable guy.
un farfallone.	a Casanova.
un bastardo.	a bastard.
un gigolò.	a gigolo.
un animale da letto.	a sex animal. (Literally: an animal for bed)
una macchina da sesso.	a sex machine.
uno sciupafemmine.	a male slut.

This popular word is a combo of "sciupare", to spoil or ruin, and "femmine", female.

safe sex

Be careful! You'll probably need these:

Hai un...?
preservativo
guanto (Literally: glove)
goldone
cappuccio (Literally: hood)

Do you have a <u>condom</u>?

Prendi la pillola?
Are you on the pill?

Hai il diaframma?
Did you put the diaphragm in?

Hai la spirale?
Do you use an IUD?

STDs 101

Don't get caught with your pants down.

Quella tipa ha...	She has...
una malattia venerea.	a venereal disease.
la sifilide.	syphillis.
l'aids.	AIDS.
l'herpes.	herpes.
l'epatite c.	hepatitis C.

Make sure you ask...

– **Hai fatto il test per l'aids?** Have you had an AIDS test?
– **Certo, tutto a posto!** Sure! Everything's OK!

GAY and LESBIAN LIFE

Looking for fun in all the alternative places? Look no further.

- *terms for gays and lesbians*
- *all about gay culture*

is he gay?

Whether you're gay or have a friend who is, here's the language you need to talk about homosexuality.

Franco è…   Franco is…
omosessuale.   homosexual.
gay.   gay.
diverso.   "different".

Maurizio è…
frocio.
This was once an offensive term, but is now used by the gay community.
finocchio. (Literally: fennel)
An old-fashioned term usually said by older folks, but it's still used.
ricchione. (Literally: big ear)
Also spelled "recchione"; it comes from Naples, but is known everywhere.
un culattone.
The word, mainly used in northern Italy, comes from "culo", ass.
un busone. VENETO, EMILIA
(Literally: big ass[hole])
un checca.

Maurizio is <u>gay</u>.

Katia è lesbica.
Katia is a lesbian.
Warning! If used in the wrong context, all of these terms can be derogatory.

 Italy is mainly a Catholic country and, therefore, homosexuality is—for the most part—still taboo. The more liberal Italian towns are often tolerant of gay lifestyles. Bologna is considered the "gay capital" of Italy. Many gay-friendly locations can also be found throughout Rome and its suburbs. Milan is another city in which gay bars and clubs thrive. For gay guys and lesbians who want to relax, try Versilia, an area in Tuscany which is gay-friendly; the same can be said about the coast of Romagna.

gay pride

Some colorful vocabulary about unconventional lifestyles.

Andrea è dell'altra sponda.
Andrea is from the other side. (Literally: Andrea is from the other riverbank.)

Gli piacciono gli uomini.
He likes men.

Fabio è andato via con il suo nuovo amichetto.
Fabio left with his new gay partner. (Literally: Fabio left with his little friend.)

Luca è troppo effemminato.
Luca is so effeminate.

Le piacciono le donne.
She likes women.

È una maschiaccia.
She's a tomboy.

È sicuramente una lesbo.
She is definitely a lesbo.

alternative places

Find that fun gay hangout.

Conosci…	Do you know…
una discoteca gay?	a gay dance club?
una discoteca lesbo?	a lesbian dance club?
un pub gay?	a gay bar?

is he or she bi?

È bisex.
He/She is bi.

Le piace provare di tutto.
He/She likes to try everything.

Le piace andare sia con gli uomini che con le donne.
She likes to go both ways. (Literally: She likes to go with both men and women.)

Maurizio è un vero metrosessuale.
Maurizio is a real metrosexual.

 Think that metrosexuals exist only in New York and London? The trend is getting popular everywhere, including places like Florence, Milan, and Rome. The typical Italian metrosexual is male, a very snappy dresser, knows about everything designer (especially Italian), and—is heterosexual! Seems unbelievable, girls, but it's true. This guy is everything you've wanted in a boyfriend with one very important fringe benefit: he'll go shopping with you. Things may get messy, though, when his wardrobe gets better than yours…

SPORTS and GAMES

From the stadium to the gym, on the field or behind the joystick, don't let anybody make sport of your Italian.

- ◆ *cheer for your team and insult the opposition*
- ◆ *talk about the coolest sports*
- ◆ *work up a sweat about gym language*
- ◆ *toy around with video-game lingo*
- ◆ *get in on the gambling action*

cheers

Hey sports fans—motivate the players with these.

Forza Juve!
Go for it Juve!
"Juve" is one of Italy's national soccer teams.

Forza Milan alè alè!
Go for it Milan! Cheer up!

Vai così!
Go this way!

Tira!
Throw (the ball)!

Passala!
Pass (the ball)!
Do it!!!

Siamo solo noi.
We are the champions.
This refers to a famous song by Vasco Rossi.

È uno spettacolo.
What a performance. (Literally: It's a spectacle.)
Amazing, wasn't it?!

Facci sognare!
Make us dream!

 In Italy people will scream anything to motivate their team—they've even been known to personalize songs about their favorite team or players. A very popular song in Rome is "Ma che siete venuti a fa'?" *What did you come for?* What they *really* mean is: You came to lose!

compliments

Use these expressions to celebrate your team's spectacular moves and shots.

Che partita!
What a move!

È stata una partita…!	It was a/an…move!
favolosa	fabulous
fantastica	fantastic
mitica	amazing (Literally: mythical)
indimenticabile	unforgettable
unica	unique
da paura	terrific

È stato un goal…	It was a/an…goal.
della Madonna.	wonderful (Literally: from the Madonna)
divino.	heavenly (Literally: divine)
spettacolare.	spectacular

Ha giocato…	He played…
da Dio.	like a god.
divinamente.	divinely.
da fuoriclasse.	like a champion.

Un attacco formidabile!
An amazing attack!

Se la sono sudata.
They had to sweat to win.

Ce la siamo meritata!
We earned it!

È stato/a…!	It was…!
un partitone	a great game
una gran partita	
una partita storica	an historic game
la partita del secolo	the game of the century

insults

Harrassing the referee and humiliating the opponent is part of your job as a spectator.

Arbitro cornuto!
Referee, you're a sucker! (Literally: Referee, you're a cuckold!)

Arbitro venduto!
Referee, you sold yourself!

Che arbitro del cazzo!
What a @#&!ng referee!

Arbitro bastardo!
Referee, you're a bastard!

Ma che cazzo fai, coglione?!
What the @#&! are you doing, dick?!

Un-Censored

Love soccer, "calcio"? A soccer game is the perfect scenario to use all the dirty words you know. Here is a good selection; we suggest you use them inside the stadium only.

Figlio di puttana!
Son of a bitch!

Stronzo!
Turd!

Pezzo di merda!
Piece of shit!

Vaffanculo!
@#&! off!

abuses

Frustrated because your team is losing? Try these.

Tira quella cazzo di palla! 🌡
Throw that @#&!ing ball!

Sei un coglione! 🌡
You dick! (Literally: You're a testicle!)

Cazzo, tirala in porta! 🌡
Shit, kick at the goal!

Corri in difesa!
Get on defense!

Marcalo stretto!
Play tight defense! (Literally: Score tight!)

Che cappella! 🌡
What a @#&!-up!

got game?

Ti piace…?	Do you like…?
il baseball	baseball
il basket	basketball
la box	boxing
la formula 1	Formula 1
il ciclismo	cycling
il rugby	rugby
il monopattino	skateboarding
il pattinaggio inline	inline skating

l'atletica leggera	track and field
la pallavolo	volleyball
il sollevamento pesi	weightlifting
le arti marziali	martial arts
il surf	surfing
il windsurf	windsurfing
il kite-surf	kitesurfing
il nuoto	swimming
la pallanuoto	water polo
lo sci nautico	water skiing
lo sci	skiing
lo snowboard	snowboarding

working out

Get active! Exercise your Italian fitness vocabulary.

Vado…	I go…
in palestra.	to the gym.
a fare un po' di movimento.	exercising. (Literally: move myself a bit)
ad aerobica.	to do aerobics.
a far pesi.	to lift weights.
a fare body building.	body building.
a fare gag.	to do the BLT workout.
	BLT = butt, legs, tummy
a fare spinning.	spinning.
a fare un po' di cyclette.	to use the fitness bike.
a fare un po' di tapis roulant.	to use the treadmill.
a fare acqua gym.	to do water aerobics.

Dai che ce la fai!
Come on! You can do it!

Ancora uno sforzo!
One more try!

Non ce la faccio più!
I'm exhausted!

Sono…	I'm…
esausto/a.	exhausted.
sfinito/a.	run-down.
stanco/a.	tired.
morto/a.	dead.
arrivato/a.	done. (Literally: arrived)
cotto/a.	fried. (Literally: cooked)

Sto sudando come un cammello!
The sweat is pouring out of me! (Literally: I'm sweating like a camel!)

gym extras

Don't forget about these gym benefits.

Avete…?	Do you have…?
la sauna	a sauna
il bagno turco	a steam room
la doccia	a shower
i massaggi	massage service
Non dimenticare…	Don't forget…
i pantaloncini.	the shorts.
la maglietta.	the T-shirt.
l'asciugamano.	the towel.
la tuta.	the leotard and leggings.

fun & games

Video game lingo at its best.

Facciamo una partita alla play?
Want to play with PlayStation®?

Facciamo un doppio?
Should we play together?

Colpiscilo!
Get him!

Sparagli!
Shoot at him!

Becca il fantasma!
Get the ghost!

Fallo fuori!
Kill him!

L'ho steso!
I hit him!

L'ho ammazzato!
I killed him!

L'ho abbattuto!
I knocked him down!

Though home video games are gaining in popularity throughout Italy, board and card games are still as hot as ever. Many Italians love to socialize and would rather play group games than stay at home with their video games. In fact, a number of trendy bars keep board games on hand for their customers.

gambling

Practice these expressions before you put your money down and risk it all.

Hai già puntato?
Did you place your bet?

Su chi hai puntato?
On what did you bet?

Ho puntato 100€ sul rosso.
I bet 100€ on red.

Ho fatto 13!
I got 13!
Think this is a bad thing? It's not! See the FACT, below.

Ho vinto la lotteria!
I won the lottery!

Ho avuto un culo della Madonna!
I was really lucky! (Literally: I had a great ass!)

Mi hanno fottuto!
They @#&!ed me!

Sono rovinato/a.
I'm ruined.

Ho la sfiga che mi perseguita.
Luck is against me.

FACT Italians have combined the best of two worlds: sports and gambling. "Totocalcio" is a national soccer lottery game; simply fill in the coupon with the teams you think will win. If you manage to get the goal of 14 points, you're awarded a cash prize. A smaller prize is also awarded to those who get 13 points. Another popular game is the virtual "Fantacalcio". You create your own team with current players and organize your own championships. The results are based on how your players perform during the real matches!

SHOPPING

*G*et ready to shop till you drop.

- ◆ shop like a pro
- ◆ make a deal and bargain with the best of 'em

shopping savvy

Use these questions to help you get around Italy's stores and shops.

Dov'è il reparto…?	Where is the…department?
donne / uomini	women's / men's
articoli sportivi	sportswear
costumi da bagno	swimwear
calzature	shoe
profumeria	cosmetics
Cercavo qualcosa di…	I'm looking for something…
sobrio.	simple. (Literally: sober)
elegante.	elegant.
sportivo.	sporty.
carino.	cute.
sfizioso.	special.
provocante.	provocative, sexy.
originale.	original, unique.

the scoop

Italy is a shopping paradise. Do you love fashion? Then you should visit Milan for high fashion or Florence for top-quality merchandise. Love shoes? Visit the beautiful Marche, a region known all over the world for their quality leather shoes. Are cars your passion? Take a tour of the famous Ferrari Museum in Maranello. Want the best souvenirs? Drop in on Venice, during Carnival perhaps, and pick up some authentic masks and other Venetian handicrafts. Don't forget that Viareggio also has an historic Carnival; you can find top quality souvenirs there as well. Looking for the best deal? Just about every major Italian brand has a factory outlet store, "spaccio aziendale". You'll get deep discounts on everything from designer hats to famous footwear.

let's go shopping!

Grab your wallet along with this essential list of shoppers' questions and phrases.

Hai anche taglie più grandi?
Do you have bigger sizes?

Hai la 42?
Do you have size 42?

Hai anche altri colori?
Do you have it in other colors?

No, non è il mio genere / stile.
No, it's not my style.

Cercavo qualcosa di più giovanile.
I was looking for something more youthful.

Posso provare questo paio di pantaloni?
Could I try on these pants?

Dov'è lo spogliatoio?
Where is the fitting room?

Dove avete…?	Where can I find…?
i CD	CDs
i DVD	DVDs
le cartoline	postcards
i libri	books
giornali e riviste	newspapers and magazines

 In Italy, shops aren't the only places where you can buy clothes and other merchandise. There are tons of unique markets in big cities and villages alike. In Rome there is the famous "Porta Portese". Here, you can find just about everything: from food and drink to clothes and accessories. You can also find the latest fashions by Italy's top designers. But beware: a lot of the designer items you'll find at these markets are knock-offs!

let's talk shop

Here are some typical sentences every sales clerk will use to tempt you.

Posso aiutarti?
Can I help you?

Posso esserti utile?
Can I help you? (Literally: Can I be of help?)

Cercavi qualcosa in particolare?
Are you looking for something in particular?

Vuoi vedere qualcos'altro?
Do you want to see anything else?

Se hai bisogno chiedi pure!
If you need something, please ask me!

 Confronted by an annoying sales clerk?

– Ciao! Posso aiutarti? Hi! Can I help you?
– No, davo solo un'occhiata in giro. No, I'm just looking around.

pay up

Looking to part with your hard-earned dough? Here's the lingo you need to make your purchase.

Quanto costa?
How much is it?

Quanto viene?
How much is it? (Literally: How much does it come?)
A familiar way to ask.

Posso pagare con il bancomat?
Can I pay with a bank / debit card?

Posso pagare con la carta di credito?
Can I pay with a credit card?

Accettate assegni?
Do you accept checks?

Non facciamo credito.
No layaway given.

money, money, money

Need some?

Mi presti…?
un po' di soldi
un po' di quattrini
(Literally: some pennies)   Can you lend me some <u>money</u>?
due verdoni (Literally: two
big bills)

what a steal

You can bank on success with these expressions.

Facciamo 10€ e non se ne parla più?
Let's make it 10€ and drop it? (Literally: Should we make it 10€ and not speak of it any longer?)
Use your bargaining power!

Mi vuoi rovinare?
Do you want to ruin me?

È stato un affare!
It was a bargain!

Quel negozio ha dei prezzi niente male.
That shop's prices aren't bad.
Reminder to self: go here again!

Quel negozio ha della bella roba.
That shop has good stuff.

Mi è costato un occhio della testa!
It cost me an arm and a leg! (Literally: It cost me an eye from my head!)

È un furto!
It's a total rip-off!

Mi è costato lo stipendio!
It cost my entire salary!

Mi hanno salassato.
They robbed me. (Literally: They fleeced me.)

In quel negozio sono cari ammazzati!
That shop is deathly expensive!

FASHION

It's true: Italians are the ultimate fashionistas. And attire isn't the only fashion to be followed—there are chic hairstyles, hobbies, and attitudes!

- *gossip about somebody's style or lack of it*
- *name all the clothes in your ultra chic wardrobe*
- *experience an Italian "beauty farm"*
- *prep for a good hair day*
- *enhance your knowledge of body alterations*

got the look?

Are your clothes hot—or not?

Questi pantaloni…	These pants…
sono fighi.	are cool.
sono un tot fighi. NORTHERN ITALY	are really cool.
sono una figata.	are cool.
sono troppo belli.	are so nice. (Literally: too nice)
sono all'ultimo grido.	are stylish. (Literally: in the latest shout)
sono alla moda.	are in fashion.
sono in / out.	are in / out.
sono passati di moda.	are out of fashion.
sono da zia.	are old-fashioned. (Literally: in the style of my aunt)
fanno schifo.	are gross.
Quella gonna…	That skirt…
ti sta da Dio!	looks divine on you!
sembra fatta apposta per te.	was made for you.
sembra fatta su misura per te.	looks custom-made for you.
ti sta troppo bene.	totally suits you.
t'ingrassa.	makes you look fat.
ti fa più magra.	is thinning.
Francesca…	Francesca…
è troppo alla moda.	is so fashionable.
si veste figa.	always looks cool.
si veste troppo bene.	is always well-dressed.
si veste un po' da fighetta.	always dresses like a preppie.
si veste troppo da sfigata.	always dresses like a loser.

what to wear?

You'll find these trendy clothes in an Italian's closet. Are they in yours?

un reggiseno
bra

un top scollato
a low-cut top

un bikini
a bikini

un costume intero
swimsuit

un push-up
a push-up bra

un perizoma
a string bikini

le scarpe da tennis
sneakers

una gonna skirt

le ciabatte
slippers

una mutandina
panties

44

una giacca
a jacket

gli occhiali
glasses

un cappellino
a cap

una camicia
a shirt

un jeans
jeans

uno zaino
a backpack

**un paio
di slip**
briefs

un maglione
a sweater

le ciabatte
slippers

45

fashion victim

Got a friend without fashion sense? Make sure he knows it!

Alessandro…	Alessandro…
si veste troppo male!	is always dressed so badly!
è completamente fuori moda!	is totally out of fashion!
si veste da barbone. ♂	is dressed like a bum.

make your beauty mark

Apply these beauty expressions and you'll look—and sound—good.

Mi passi…?	Can you give me (some/a/an)…?
il fondotinta	make-up
la terra	face powder
il fard	blush
la cipria	powder
l'eyeliner	eyeliner
la matita per gli occhi	eye pencil
il correttore	concealer
l'ombretto	eye shadow
il rossetto	lipstick
il lucidalabbra	lip gloss
il burro di cacao	lip balm
il mascara	mascara
Mi servirebbe…	I need…
un pennello per il fard.	a make-up brush.
una spugnetta per il fondotinta.	a make-up sponge.
una pinzetta.	tweezers.

pamper yourself

Indulge in an Italian "beauty-farm", spa.

Vorrei...	I'd like...
un massaggio facciale.	a facial.
una ceretta completa.	a complete wax.
una ceretta nella zona bikini.	a bikini wax.
una pulizia del viso.	a face cleansing.
un massaggio anticellulite.	a cellulite massage.
un massaggio rilassante.	a relaxing massage.
farmi le unghie.	a manicure.
un pedicure.	a pedicure.
farmi le sopracciglia.	my eyebrows waxed.
fare una lampada.	a tanning session.

Italy is famous for the "beauty-farm", a place to go for skin care, treatments, and massage. Some are day-spas and others are hotel spas, where guests can be pampered all weekend—if not longer!

 Looking for a cure-all or just want some rest and relaxation? Visit an Italian spa or resort that features a hot water spring and enjoy luxury treatments like massage or mud therapy alongside your dip into the thermal baths. Proponents say that the thermal water can help cure respiratory problems, skin conditions, arthritis, and more. Just keep in mind that water temperatures can reach almost 37.7 degrees C—that's 100 degrees F!

let your hair down

From cut to curls, find the language you need for the hairstyle you want.

Hai un parrucchiere di fiducia da consigliarmi?
Can you recommend a good hair stylist?

Vorrei…	I'd like…
farmi una tinta.	to dye my hair.
farmi un riflesso.	some highlights.
farmi le mèches.	some streaks in my hair.
tagliarmi i capelli.	a hair cut.

Me li stiri con la piastra?
Can you flat iron my hair?

Mi fai un taglio scalato?
Can you layer my hair?

Vorrei farmi una messa in piega.
I'd like to have my hair styled.
This orginally meant set in rollers!

Sai dov'è un barbiere?
Do you know where the barber shop is?

Li vorrei rasati.
I'd like to have my head shaved.

Mi piace quel ragazzo…	I like that boy…
con i capelli ricci.	with curly hair.
rasato.	with shaved head.
biondo.	with blonde hair.
moro.	with dark hair.
con i capelli castani.	with brown hair.
con i capelli rossi.	with red hair.

in the bathroom

Don't forget those toiletry essentials—just keep your language fresh and clean.

For him…

Dove posso trovare…?	Where can I find…?
un rasoio	a razor
della crema da barba	some shaving cream
del dopobarba	some aftershave
del gel	some hair gel
del profumo	some cologne

For her…

Hai…?	Do you have…?
una pastiglia per i dolori mestruali	pills for cramps
un assorbente	a pad
un tampone	a tampon
un po' di crema per le mani	some hand cream
del profumo	some perfume

body alterations

Fashion is more than just the right clothes. You've got to have the right body too.

È completamente rifatta!
She is totally re-made!
Meaning: She's had a ton of plastic surgery.

Si è rifatta…	She had… (Literally: She remade…)
il seno.	a boob job.
il naso.	a nose job.
il doppiomento.	a "double chin" removed.
il fondoschiena.	butt surgery. *Implants or liposuction.*

Si è fatta un lifting al viso.
She had a face lift.

Si è siliconata…	She enhanced her…
le tette.	boobs.
le labbra.	lips.
le chiappe.	butt.

Ha il piercing…	He/She has a/an…piercing.
all'ombelico.	belly button
al sopracciglio.	eyebrow
sul capezzolo.	nipple
al naso.	nose
sul mento.	chin
lì.	genital (Literally: there)

È tatuato.
He's got a tattoo.

Ha un tatuaggio troppo figo.
He/She has a cool tattoo.

BODY

*T*he bare facts—from head to toe.

- ◆ speak up about body parts and body image
- ◆ let loose—talk about burping, farting, and other gross stuff

body beautiful

Here's the skinny on that perfect—or not so perfect—Italian body.

Anna ha... — Anna has…
un gran fisico. — a great body.
un fisico della Madonna. — an incredible body. *By now, you're really familiar with the slang term "Madonna".*

un gran telaio — a great frame.
una bella carrozzeria. — a good structure.
un fisico mozzafiato. — a breathtaking body.
un corpo da far girar la testa. — a body that makes your head spin.
un fisichetto niente male. — a nice body.
due gran tette. — nice boobs.
due bocce favolose. — fabulous boobs. (Literally: fabulous bowls)

un culo bello sodo. — a firm butt.
due gambe da favola. — fabulous legs.

Fabio ha... — Fabio has…
un fondoschiena niente male. — a nice backside.
un gran fisico. — a great body.
dei gran muscoli. — good muscles.
la tartaruga. — a six-pack. (Literally: the tortoise)
un fisico da palestrato. — a sculpted body. *"Palestrato" comes from "palestra", gym.*

la panza da birra. — a beer belly.
una gran trippa. — a big belly. (Literally: a big tripe)
dei gran rotoli. — big rolls.

butt ugly

For those that don't look their best, use these.

Giovanna è fatta a pera.

Giovanna is shaped like a pear.

Not a positive trait...

Anna è praticamente quadrata.

Anna is shapeless. (Literally: Anna is practically square-shaped).

Ouch!

Serena è una tavola da surf.

Serena is a surfboard.

She's that flat?!

Stefania è una botte.

Stefania is fat. (Literally: Stefania is a barrel.)

Marco è un ciccione.

Marco is a fattie.

"Ciccione" comes from the word "ciccia", which is what children use to say meat.

Luisa è...	Luisa is...
cicciottella / rotondetta.	chubby.
grossa.	fat. (Literally: big)
ben piazzata / robusta.	robust. *A nice way to state the obvious.*
in carne.	well-padded. (Literally: fleshy)

body parts

Body parts don't have to be private!

> | *Warning! Some of the language on this page can be pretty hot!*

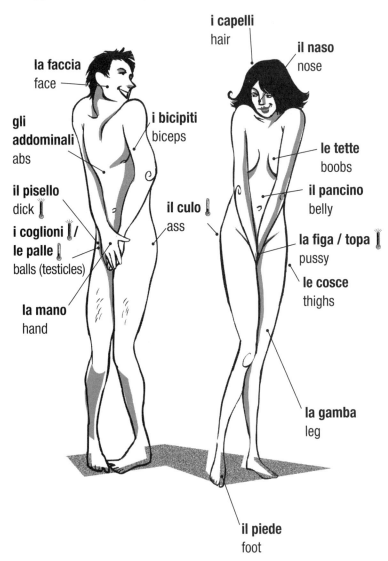

i capelli
hair

il naso
nose

la faccia
face

gli addominali
abs

i bicipiti
biceps

le tette
boobs

il pisello
dick |

il pancino
belly

il culo |
ass

i coglioni | /
le palle |
balls (testicles)

la figa / topa |
pussy

le cosce
thighs

la mano
hand

la gamba
leg

il piede
foot

skin problems

Mi è spuntato un brufolo sul naso!
I got a pimple on my nose!

Sono pieno/a di brufoli!
I'm full of pimples!

Sono pieno/a di punti neri!
I'm full of blackheads!

Mi puzzano le ascelle / i piedi.
My armpits / feet stink.

Ho dei peli che sembro un orso!
I'm as hairy as a bear!

body functions

Vado alla toilette.
I'm going to the toilet.

Vado in bagno.
I'm going to the bathroom.

Vado a fare la pipì / popò.
I'm going to pee / poop.

Vado a fare la cacca.
I'm going to take a crap.

Vado a cagare.
I'm going to take a shit.

Vado in seduta.
I'm going to a session.
Meaning: You'll be in the restroom for some time.

Devo andare di corpo.
I need to poop. (Literally: I need to give from the body.)

gross

Totally nasty…

Qualcuno ha fatto uno scoreggione!
Someone farted!

Chi ha fatto una puzzetta?
Who farted? (Literally: Who made a small stink?)

Ha fatto un rutto!
He/She burped!

Che schifo! Hai una caccola nel naso!
That's gross! You have a snot in your nose!

Bleah! Hai i brustolini negli occhi.
Ew! You have goo in your eyes.

Hai qualcosa in mezzo ai denti.
You have something in your teeth.

Hai un brufolone pieno di pus proprio sul naso.
You have a big pimple full of pus on your nose.

Dai, non schiacciarti i brufoli!
Don't squeeze those pimples!

Ha un alito che ti stende!
He/She has toxic breath!

Ha l'alito pesante!
He/She has bad breath! (Literally: He/She has heavy breath!)

Help out a friend in need.

– **Hai qualcosa in mezzo ai denti!** You have something in your teeth!

– **Davvero? Che imbarazzo!** Really? That's so embarassing!

– **Tieni… uno stuzzicadente.** Here's a toothpick.

sick!

Not feeling your best today?

Ahiaiai, ho…
Ugh! I have…

la diarrea.
diarrhea.

la caghetta. 🌡
the runs. *"Caghetta" is the diminutive of "cacca", poop.*

il mal di mare.
motion sickness.

il mal d'aria.
air sickness.

il mal di stomaco.
stomach pains.

dei crampi terribili.
terrible cramps.

la febbre.
a fever.

l'influenza.
the flu.

il raffreddore.
a cold.

la tosse.
a cough.

Sto di merda. 🌡
I feel like shit.

Sto uno schifo.
I feel gross.

Ho un mal di testa atroce.
I have an atrocious headache.

Sto morendo dal dolore.
The pain is killing me.

Non hai una gran bella cera oggi.
You don't look well today.

Hai un faccino così sbattuto!
You look awful! (Literally: You have such a small face!)

TECHNOLOGY

*C*ompute Italian technology talk with ease.

- ◆ *process computer lingo and netspeak*
- ◆ *communicate by e-mail or in chat rooms*
- ◆ *speak on the phone*
- ◆ *use text messaging shorthand*

log on

A little tech talk in Italian.

Accendi il computer.
Turn on the computer.

Posso connettermi con il tuo computer?
Can I connect (to the internet) on your computer?

Posso controllare le mie mail?
Can I check my e-mail?

Posso scaricare della roba?
Can I download some stuff?

Sono in rete / online.
I'm on the web / online.

Zippa / Comprimi quel file.
Compress that file.

Apri / Chiudi il documento.
Open / Close the document.

Cancellalo.
Delete it.

L'hai salvato?
Did you save it?

Clicca qui!
Click here!

 Looking for some computer help?

– **Non riesco ad aprire la mia posta.** I can't open my mail.
– **Vuoi che ti aiuti?** Do you want me to help you?
– **Grazie!** Thank you!

e-mail

In need of a translation?

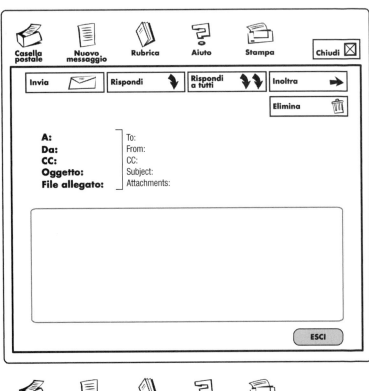

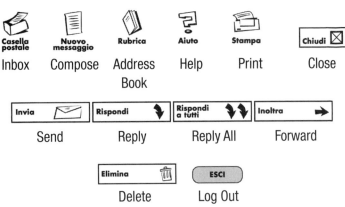

Inbox	Compose	Address Book	Help	Print	Close

Send	Reply	Reply All	Forward

Delete	Log Out

help desk

Problems with your computer? Here are a few expressions that could help you.

Il computer...	The computer...
si è bloccato.	froze. (Literally: is blocked)
non dà segni di vita.	doesn't show any signs of life.
non risponde.	doesn't answer.
si è impallato.	is frozen.
è morto.	died.

Il file è...	The file is...
andato perso.	lost.
stato danneggiato.	damaged.
stato eliminato.	deleted.
fottuto.	@#&!ed.

You've got big problems, eh?!

FACT Many people in Italy who don't have personal computers visit Internet cafés, where they check their e-mail and chat. Some of these cafés are cool places to meet Internet-savvy friends and foreigners while enjoying light refreshments—from espresso to beer.

the Scoop

Looking for some on-line lovin'? Romance rooms are among the most popular. If you'd like to get hot and heavy on-line, you should know these phrases:

Sono un ragazzo / una ragazza...
I'm a girl / guy...

in cerca di un ragazzo / una ragazza...
looking for a guy / a girl...

tra i xx e xx anni...
between xx and xx years old...

a cui piace...
who likes...

Mandami una e-mail all'indirizzo...
Write to me at...

communicate on-line

E-mail or chat in Italian.

Stai navigando?
Are you surfing?

Ho trovato un sito che è una figata!
I found a cool website!

È il mio sito preferito.
It's my favorite website.

Puoi mandarmi il link?
Can you send me the link?

Mi piace un sacco chattare!
I love to chat!

Mi dai la tua mail?
Can you give me your e-mail?

Hai un indirizzo e-mail?
Do you have an e-mail address?

Non guardare la mia password!
Don't look at my password!

pick up the phone!

Is the phone ringing? Want to call someone? Don't freak out! Use these...

Dove ho messo il mio cellulare / telefonino?
Where did I put my cell phone?
"Telefonino" literally means little phone.

Pronto?
Hello? (Literally: Ready?)

Sì?

Yes?

Chi parla?

Who's speaking?

Mi passi Alessandro per favore?

May I speak with Alessandro please? (Literally: Can you give me Alessandro please?)

C'è Rosa?

Is Rosa there?

Posso parlare con Anna?

Can I speak with Anna?

Sono io!

It's me!

Aspetta un attimo che te la passo.

Hold on a moment, she's coming. (Literally: Wait a moment, I'll give her to you.)

Un attimo solo.

Just a moment.

Non è in casa, la trovi più tardi.

She's not in, you can catch her later.

Chiamami!

Call me!

Fatti sentire!

Let me hear from you!

Fammi uno squillo più tardi!

Call me later! (Literally: Give me a ring later!)

Leave a message—in Italian.

– Ciao, lasciate un messaggio dopo il bip! Hi! Leave a message after the beep!
– Ciao, sono Luca, mi richiami? Hi, this is Luca; call me back?

get off the phone

Learn your phone manners and hang up with grace.

Scusa ma devo andare.
Excuse me, but I have to go.

Devo scappare!
I must be off!

Scusa, c'è mia madre che mi sta chiamando!
Excuse me, my mother is calling me!
When all else fails, use this tactic to get off the phone!

Ci sentiamo più tardi?
Can we speak later? (Literally: Can we hear from each other later?)

Me lo mandi un bacio prima di riattaccare?
Will you send me a kiss before you hang up?

It seems that just about everyone in Italy—adults, teens, and kids—has a wireless phone. Some even have two! Though making and receiving calls remains fairly expensive, it's one of the most popular forms of communication. Wireless phones are so popular that it's important to personalize them with unique colors, designs, and even ring tones, "suonerie".

text messaging

Some short and sweet text messages.

Dove 6? [Dove sei?]
Where are you?
"Sei" the number six is spelled the same as "sei", you are.

Ki 6? [Chi sei?]
Who are you?

C sent + tardi! [Ci sentiamo più tardi!]
Let's talk later.

C ved dopo! [Ci vediamo dopo!]
CUL8TR [See you later.]

M. bene [Molto bene]
very well

Abb. bene [Abbastanza bene]
pretty good

Tr. tardi [Troppo tardi]
too late

Nn so [Non so]
I don't know.

Xké nn 6 venuto? [Perchè non sei venuto?]
Why didn't you come?

TVTB [Ti Voglio Tanto Bene]
I love you very much.
Used by friends and lovers.

TAT [Ti Amo Tanto]
I love you so much.

10 GOSSIP

What to say—good and bad—about family and friends.

- ◆ *gossip about people you love and hate*
- ◆ *learn to keep a secret*
- ◆ *insult an enemy*
- ◆ *talk about your family*

best friends

Haven't you met the nicest people in Italy?

Ha un cuore grande!
You've got a big heart!
This person will do anything for a friend.

È un tesoro.
He/She's a sweetheart. (Literally: He/She's a treasure.)
Your friend's got a heart of gold, huh?!

È proprio una brava persona.
He/She's a really sweet person.
Too bad there aren't more people like this in the world!

È veramente forte.
He/She's really solid. (Literally: He/She's really strong.)
You can always count on this person in a pinch.

È mitico / un mito!
He/She's a legend! (Literally: He/She's a myth!)
Everyone knows how cool this person is!

È troppo avanti.
He/She's such a trendsetter. (Literally: He/She's too advanced.)
Make sure you follow this person's lead...

È troppo figo/a.
He/She's so cool.
Hope you know a lot of people like this!

ex-friends

Is he or she the most annoying person you've ever met? Say it!

È proprio un bel tipo!
He/She's really something!
Meant sarcastically, of course.

Non lo sopporto quel figlio di papà!
I can't stand that momma's boy! (Literally: I can't stand that daddy's son!)
You'll notice the extra accusative "lo" in there—it's not grammatically correct, but everyone says it!

Anna non mi sta per niente simpatica.
I don't like Anna at all.

Non la posso vedere / soffrire / digerire!
I can't stand her! (Literally: I can't see / stand / digest her!)

Mi sta sulle scatole!
He/She ticks me off! (Literally: He/She is on my boxes!)

Mi sta sulle balle!
He/She pisses me off! (Literally: He/She is on my balls!)
You're really annoyed, huh?!

Mi sta troppo sul cazzo / sui coglioni!
He/She is a dick! (Literally: He/She is on my dick / balls!)
You've totally had it with this person!

È un povero sfigato.
He's a sore loser.

Mi urta i nervi.
He/She gets on my nerves.
You've had enough of this person, huh?!

gossip

Have you heard the latest scandal? Share your shock with your friends.

Ho una news fenomenale!
I've got incredible news!

Ho una notizia bomba!
I have a real bomb!

Sai cos'è successo…?
Ya know what happened…?

Senti questa…
Listen to this…

Non ci crederai, ma…
You won't believe it, but…

La sai l'ultima?!
Heard the latest?

hush hush

Confide in your friends—but make sure your secrets remain untold.

Lo sai mantenere un segreto?
Can you keep a secret?

Acqua in bocca.
Keep it quiet. (Literally: Water in mouth.)

Che rimanga tra noi…
Keep it between the two of us…

Che rimanga tra queste quattro mura…
Keep it within these walls…

Muto come un pesce!
Quiet as a mouse! (Literally: As silent as a fish!)

Portatelo nella tomba.
Take it to the tomb.

spreading rumors

Pointing out the faults of other people can be an entertaining pastime.

Annalisa è...	Annalisa is...
una che non vale niente.	worthless.
una gran sfigata.	a big loser.
una gran pettegola.	a big gossip.
la principessa sul pisello. ♀	a princess. (Literally: the princess on the pea)
uno scaricatore di porto.	totally vulgar. (Literally: a docker)

annoying acquaintances

Time to gossip about those annoying people you know.

È...	She is...
maliziosa.	bitchy.
cattiva.	mean.
dispettosa.	spiteful.
perfida.	evil.
Ivano è...	Ivano is...
un gran imbecille.	a big imbecile.
un chiacchierone.	a gossip.
un fannullone.	a lazy bum.
uno stupido.	a stupid guy.
un idiota / cazzaro.	an idiot.
un cazzone.	a dick.

temper, temper

Pissed off at someone? Get the anger out.

Non la reggo / sopporto!
I can't stand / take her!

La ucciderei!
I would kill her!

Mi fa una rabbia…
It pissed me off so much…

Sto per scoppiare dalla rabbia!
I'm ready to explode (with anger)!

Ho un incazzo addosso che l'ammazzerei!
I'm so angry that I could kill her/him!

shut up!

How do you get someone to stop bullshitting? Try these…

Taci!
Shut up!

Ma stà zitto/a che è meglio!
Shut up, it's better for you!

Non prendermi in giro!
Don't tease me!

Non prendermi per il culo!
Don't @#&! with me! (Literally: Don't take me from my ass!)

Smettila di dire…
cavolate.
baggianate.
cazzate.
stronzate.

Stop bullshitting.

cool down

Got a friend who's in a bad way? Offer some words of comfort.

Stai calmo!
Keep calm!

Calmati! Non vale la pena!
Calm down! It isn't worth the worry!

Non farci caso.
Don't worry about it.

Lascialo perdere.
Don't pay attention to him. (Literally: Leave him alone.)

Non dargli retta!
Don't listen to him!

Non badarci! / Fregatene!
Screw it!

Un-Censored

Use these to really insult someone.

Vai all'inferno!
Go to the hell!

Vai a quel paese!
Go to hell! (Literally: Go to that village!)

Vai a cagare!
Go take a shit!

Vai a farti fottere!
@#&! you!

Vaffanculo!
@#&! off!

Sparisci!
Disappear!

Un-Censored

And use these if you've just been insulted.

Sei una testa di cazzo!
You dickhead!

Tua madre!
Your mother!

Figlio di buona donna!
Son of a bitch! (Literally: Son of a good woman!)

Figlio di puttana!
Son of a bitch!

Non me ne frega un cazzo / una sega!
I don't give a @#&!! (Literally: I don't give a dick / masturbation!)

family slang

Ci tengo molto…	I care a lot about…
i miei.	my parents.
i miei vecchi.	my parents. (Literally: my old ones)
la mia vecchia.	my old lady.
la mia mammina.	my little mom.
la mia mammona.	my big mom.
la mia mami.	my mom.
il mio vecchio.	my old man.
il mio papi.	my pop.
il mio babbo.	my daddy.
il mio papà.	my dad.

FOOD

*F*resh Italian language about food and other delicious goodies.

◆ *say that you're hungry*
◆ *say it's yummy or yucky*
◆ *turn down junk food*
◆ *talk about bad eating habits*

the big bite

The best slang terms about food.

Ad Antonio piace molto…
magnare.* ROME
pappare.
sbocconcellare. (Literally: nibbling)
ingozzarsi. (Literally: stuffing himself)

Antonio loves <u>eating</u>.

Ho una fame da lupi.
I'm as hungry as a wolf.

Se non mangio, svengo!
If I don't eat, I'll faint!

Ho una fame che mangerei un bue.
I'm so hungry that I could eat an ox.

Cosa non darei per un gelato.
I would give anything for an ice cream.

Sto morendo di sete.
I'm dying of thirst.

Sono disidratato.
I'm dehydrated.

Italians know how to eat well. Fast food joints offer goodies such as: "pizza"; "piadina", stuffed pizza; "gnocchi", potato dumplings; "tigella", rice croquettes; and other kinds of "stuzzicherie", snacks. Even though you can eat pretty well at an Italian fast food stand, going out for a sit-down meal at a nice restaurant is very popular—there's often live music to enjoy along with great wine and cocktails.

* *"Magnare", from "mangiare", means eating, in Rome; elsewhere it means eating a lot.*

yummy or yucky?

Is that meal good—or gross?

Mmh! Che buono!
Mmm! Really good!

È delizioso / squisito!
It's delicious!

È buonissimo!
It's so good!

È una prelibatezza!
It's deliciousness!

Che schifo! 🌡
It's gross!

Ha un saporaccio.
It tastes disgusting.

Fa vomitare! 🌡
It's nasty! (Literally: It makes you vomit!)

Che merda! 🌡
What shit!

At many Italian bars, you can have just about anything: breakfast, lunch, dinner, snacks, alcoholic and non-alcoholic drinks. Most Italians go to a bar to have a quick cup of good coffee; they often just stand at the bar and drink it down in a few sips—no need to sit at a table! Bars are the coolest spot to have a cocktail and meet friends before going out on the town. Next time you're in an Italian bar, you can try a sophisticated aperitif: "mojito" (white rum, club soda, brown sugar, and mint leaves), "Negroni®" (gin, red vermouth, bitter Campari®), "caipiroska" (vodka, lime, sugar). These are all the rage right now!

overeating

Couldn't eat another bite? Say it!

Madonna, che mangiata!
God, what a good, hearty meal!

Madonna, che abbuffata!
God, what a feast!

Ho mangiato come un bue.
I ate like a pig. (Literally: I ate like an ox.)

Ho mangiato da fare schifo!
It's gross how much I ate!

Sono pieno come un uovo.
I'm full. (Literally: I'm full like an egg.)

And now?

Mi viene da…	I feel like…
rimettere.	throwing up.
vomitare.	vomiting.
dare di stomaco.	puking.

bad habits

Do your friends have bad eating habits? Tell them!

Michele mangia come un maiale. 🌡
Michele eats like a pig.

È una fogna. 🌡
He/She's a pig. (Literally: He/She's a sewer.)

È un ingordo.
He's a glutton.

Anna mangia come un uccellino / passerotto.
Anna eats like a bird / young sparrow.

FACT Calling all foodies! Here's the info you need on Italian goodies.

Have a sweet tooth? You need to taste "gianduiotti", the famous chocolate from Turin, or visit Perugia and the well-known "Perugina" chocolate house. There are also tons of small chocolatiers throughout Italy known for their handcrafted chocolates.

Love pizza? Go to the Naples region and taste the original pizza and the best mozzarella, made from buffalo's milk.

Are you a pasta freak? Italy is pasta heaven. Try some freshly made pasta with "pesto", the basil and olive oil sauce of Liguria, or sample specialty pasta like "orecchiette", pasta shaped like ears, from Puglia. Bologna and its region Emilia Romagna are a foodie's dream. There you can eat the best "lasagne", layers of pasta with cheese, meat, and tomato sauce; "tortellini", little dumplings stuffed with meat; and "tagliatelle" long, flat noodles similar to fettuccine.

Are you a wine connoisseur? Italy has one of the largest areas under vine in the world. Among the most famous wine regions are: Tuscany ("Chianti" and "Super Tuscans", red wine made from sangiovese grapes), Veneto ("grappa" and "prosecco", high-proof after-dinner drinks), and the Asti-area ("spumante", Italian champagne).

Would you die for dessert? Try "pandoro" in Verona or the "panettone" in Milan; both are favorite Christmas cakes, often available year-round.

12 PARTYING

*H*ave a bash in Italian.

- ◆ *go out and have a good time*
- ◆ *enjoy a little bubbly talk*
- ◆ *fire up your language on smoking*
- ◆ *stay out of trouble*

let's party

Be Italian—spend your weekends dancing, relaxing at the pub, or sipping drinks at a wine bar.

Andiamo a…?	Shall we (go)…?
prendere l'aperitivo	have an aperitif
ballare	dance
bere qualcosa	drink something
Conosci…?	Do you know…?
un bar carino	a nice bar
un posticino carino da consigliarmia	a nice place that's recommended?
un bel disco pub	a good club
un bel baretto	a cute little bar
qualche locale X	a hot spot (Literally: some X place)

– Ti va di uscire stasera? Do you want to go out tonight?
– Mh, dove mi porti? Hai qualche dritta per un localino carino? Hm, where will you take me? Can you recommend a nice place?
– Certo! Sure!

 **FACT** Italians start partying when they're pretty young. They hang out at local hot spots in town when they're 12 or 13 years old. At around 16, they pass the time away in dance clubs and pizzerias. Many of these clubs and pizzerias serve alcohol and, though the drinking age is officially 18, few places respect the rule.

let's drink

Feel like getting intoxicated?

Stasera ho voglia di…	Tonight I want to…
trincare.	drink. *"Trincare" is a popular expression taken from German "trinken".*
bere.	drink.
inciuccarmi.	get drunk.
sballarmi.	get drunk / high.
andare fuori.	get drunk. (Literally: go out [of one's mind])
alcolizzarmi.	get drunk.
Andiamo a…?	Should we go…?
farci l'ammazzacaffè	have a stiff drink (Literally: take a coffee killer) *You need a strong alcoholic drink to kill the sobering effects of that strong, Italian coffee, right?!*
farci un bicchiere	have a glass
bere un goccio	drink a drop
farci una birra	for a beer
scolarci una boccia di vino	drink down a bottle of wine *"Scolarci", comes from the verb "scolarsi" to drain.*
a farci un cicchettino / bicchierino	have a shot

cheers!

Don't forget to say…

Cin cin!
Cheers!

Salute!
To your health!

Alla nostra / tua / vostra!
To our / your health!
"Tua" is singular; "vostra" is plural.

Alla goccia!
To the drop!

drank too much?

Say it this way…

Francesco…
è ubriaco duro / fradicio.
  (Literally: is a hard / soaked drunk)
è bresco. BOLOGNA
si è preso una gran ciucca.
  (Literally: took a great drink)
è fuori come un balcone.
  (Literally: is out like a balcony)
è fuori come un culo. 🌡
  (Literally: is out like an ass)
è ciucco.

Francesco is <u>drunk</u>.

What's the drink of choice for young Italians? Wine, of course, is some-
what of a national drink since Italy produces some of the best. Because
wine is made in Italy, prices for a glass or bottle at a wine bar are very
reasonable. Beer—Italian or otherwise—is popular with 20-somethings.
Hipsters like to start off the evening sipping aperitifs, then spend the rest
of the evening at a pizzeria, lounging over good food and great wine.
Popular drinks at night clubs include high-proof spirits mixed with fruit
juice. Those with money to burn reserve a table at trendy clubs in order to
"be seen" with their drink of choice, champagne.

under the influence

Someone's smashed? Use these to get the message out.

Maria beve come una spugna.
Maria is a heavy drinker. (Literally: Maria drinks like a sponge.)

Ho bevuto un casino.
I drank a lot.
*"Casino" is a word that means many things: brothel, mess—but as
an adverb, like in this case, it means a lot.*

Ho bevuto da fare schifo!
I drank so much, it's gross!

Guarda che si sta inciuccando!
Look how he/she is getting drunk!

and the day after?

Ho una gran cassa. BOLOGNA
I have a big hangover. (Literally: I have a big case.)

Ho un gran cerchio alla testa.
My head is spinning. (Literally: I have a big circle around my head.)

Suffer the consequences…

– Guarda un po'! Elena è già fuori! Look! Elena is already drunk!
– Come? Di già? What? Already?

up in smoke

Puffing up is still a popular activity in Italy…

Hai…?
una sigaretta
una siga
una paglia (Literally: a straw)
da fumare (Literally: a smoke)

Do you have a <u>cigarette</u>?

Ti dà fastidio se fumo?
Do you mind if I smoke?

Te ne stai accendendo una dopo l'altra!
You're a chain smoker! (Literally: You're lighting one after the other!)

Mi fai dare due tiri?
Can I have a drag?

Smettila di fumare!
Stop smoking!

 Since 2005, smoking has been banned in public buildings —including bars, cafés, restaurants, and offices—in Italy. According to the law, smoking is allowed only in specially constructed, enclosed smoking areas. Enforcing the law, however, is a different matter. Though fines are heavy, many smokers are fuming over the law, and continue to defy it by lighting up anyway!

the high life

These expressions are for reference only.

Si è fatto/a…

una canna. (Literally: a cane)

una tromba. (Literally: a trumpet)

uno spino. (Literally: a thorn)

un joint.

He/She smoked <u>a joint</u>.

È…	He/She's…
fumato/a.	high. (Literally: smoked)
incannato/a duro.	high. (Literally: under the effect of canes)
fatto/a duro.	into drugs. (Literally: hard done)
sotto acido.	on acid.
fuori.	out.
andato/a.	gone.

Che viaggio! / È un gran viaggio!
What a trip!

Non prendo droghe.
I don't do drugs.

busted!

Hope you never need to use these expressions.

Mi sono beccato una multa per…	I got a ticket for…
eccesso di velocità.	speeding.
esser passato con il rosso.	going through a red light.
non aver rispettato lo stop.	rolling through a stop.
non aver dato la precedenza.	not giving way.

police watch

Attento! C'è la pula!
Watch out! The cops!

Occhio ai pullotti!
Watch out for cops! (Literally: Eye the cops!)

Attento, questa strada è piena di autovelox!
Watch out! There are tons of speed cameras on this road!

Occhio, qua multano di brutto!
Watch out! They give out lots of fines here!

bad endings

Ieri sera hanno fatto a botte.
Last night they had a fight.

È scattata la rissa.
There was a fight.

Hanno fatto a botte / a pugni!
They threw punches!

Mario le ha prese.
Mario was beaten up.

Lo hanno preso a cazzotti.
They punched him.

Lo hanno messo...
dentro. (Literally: inside)
in gabbia. (Literally: into the cage)
al fresco. (Literally: at the fresh)
in gattabuia. (Literally: into prison)

He got <u>arrested</u>.

ENTERTAINMENT

*B*ehind-the-scenes language on music, movies, and TV.

◆ *chill out and talk about cool tunes*
◆ *use the proper equipment*
◆ *gets the facts on Italian TV and cinema*

listen up

Get in tune to Italian sounds.

Mi piace…	I love…
la musica pop.	pop music.
il rock italiano.	Italian rock.
la musica rock.	rock music.
la musica anni '60/'70/'80.	the music of the 60s/70s/80s.
la salsa e merengue.	salsa & merengue.
la latino-americana.	Latin-American music.
il liscio.	ballroom music.
la techno.	techno.
la musica classica.	classical music.
l'house.	house.
il raggae.	reggae.
l'hip-hop.	hip-hop.
la ska.	ska.

Impazzisco per il rock.
I'm crazy about rock.

Sono un fanatico della musica classica.
I'm a classical music fanatic.

L'house mi piace un casino.
I really love house music.
Remember that word, "casino"?

live music

Did that concert rock—or not?

Sono stato ad un concerto…	I went to a…concert.
favoloso.	fabulous
spettacolare.	spectacular

meraviglioso.	great
troppo figo.	cool (Literally: too cool)
della Madonna.	great
da paura.	great (Literally: fearful)
schifoso.	awful
deludente.	disappointing
di merda.	shitty

Mi piace ascoltare la musica a palla / a manetta. NORTHERN ITALY
I like to hear music at full blast. (Literally: I like to hear music at
ball / at handcuff.)

necessary equipment

...to listen to tunes

discman
discman

la radio
radio

il lettore (di) MP3
MP3 player

le cuffie
headphones

il lettore (di) CD
CD player

le casse
speakers

il mangiacassette
cassette player

Italians listen to all kinds of music, including local and international favorites. Funny thing is, the Italian singers who are popular abroad—Eros Ramazzotti, Nek, Laura Pausini—are not so popular in Italy. Youth prefer rock. Italian bands such as Vasco Rossi, Ligabue, Piero Pelù are adored in Italy and not so well known internationally—at least, for now.

tv & movies

Learn some boob tube and big screen slang.

Mi piace un sacco...   I really like...
i cartoni animati.   cartoons.
le soap.   soaps.
il tg.   the news.
i reality show.   reality shows.
i quiz televisivi.   game shows.

Dove hai messo la guida TV?
Where did you put the TV listing?

Mi passi il telecomando?
Can you give me the remote?

Non cambiare!
Don't change (the channel)!

Ti va di andare al cinema?
What about a movie?

Ci prendiamo un video / DVD?
Should we rent a video / DVD?

film fan?

What kinds of movies are you into?

Vorrei vedere…	I'd like to see a/an…
un film d'azione.	action movie.
un film d'amore.	romance movie.
un film dell'orrore.	horror movie.
un giallo / noir.	thriller.
L'avete…	Do you have it…
in italiano?	in Italian?
in lingua originale?	in the original language?
sottotitolato?	with subtitles?

Reality-show fever has reached Italy too. People spend entire days watching them. Italians, much like people elsewhere, have a love-hate relationship with reality shows. In fact, Italians use the English word "trash" to refer to reality shows—even though so many Italians enjoy watching them!

14 GESTURES

Italians are famous all around the world for their non-verbal language—nobody can gesture like an Italian!

Cosa dici? / Ma che cazzo vuoi?
What the hell do you want?

Use this typical Italian gesture to express your annoyance.

Ma sei fuori?
Are you crazy?
(Literally: Are you out [of your mind]?)

Vaffanculo!
@#&! off!

The gesture says it all...

Ti faccio un culo cosi!
I'll make you such an ass!

This threatening gesture is used to show that someone is going to get a beating—physically or mentally.

Dimenticavo!
I forgot!

Duh!

Al bacio!
Great! (Literally: Like a kiss!)

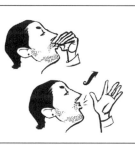

Use this gesture to show that something—or someone—is fantastic.

Che buono!
Yummy!

Delicious, right?!

93

chapter 14

I un ricchione!

He's gay! (Literally: He's a big ear!)

This is downright nasty and rude—be careful!

Ho trombato!

I had sex!

The verb "trombare" is a slang variation of the word "tromba", trumpet.

Una sega!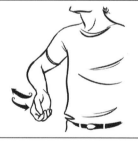

Masturbating!

You know this is a dirty gesture…!